WE CALLED HER LITTLE SISTER

Memories Worth Keeping

John E. Johnson

ISBN: 979-8-218-98503-5

Table of Contents

1 THE OVERNIGHT VISITOR

A strong wind had been relentlessly battering the old farmhouse and howling around the windows the entire day, carrying with it a threat of a heavy snowfall if a full-blown blizzard materialized. And just such a winter storm, a whiteout, had been the forecast during all weather updates on the country music radio station that dominated the airwaves throughout that area of southeastern Colorado.

Farmers all around had already acted to protect their livestock the best way they could. They were worried that their brood of hens might still have trouble surviving the temperatures outside while nesting underneath the foundation of the houses where they had been granted temporary roosting privileges. But the poorest farmers, those without enough cash money for keeping any antifreeze in the radiators of their pickup trucks and other farm vehicles and without an enclosed shed or barn to offer protection from the weather, had completely drained the radiators to prevent a freeze-up. These unprotected vehicles had all been parked close against the south side of each farmhouse in the hope, simply, that having the vehicles close in by a structure just might help shield the engine block from a solid overnight freeze if the drain plug for the block itself was inaccessible. Such a worst-case scenario freeze would be a nightmare that would require the use of a fire pan underneath the engine before it would thaw out and turn over once again to determine if the block was busted entirely or still intact for motoring into town for groceries and other supplies.

The wind had even interfered with the radio signal picked up by the battery-powered transistor radio that sat high atop the kitchen cabinet next to the wood cookstove that also functioned as the only source of heat for the entire house. A broadcast rendition of "Tumbling Tumbleweeds" by The Sons of the Pioneers had been so rudely broken up by loud, crackling static. Since that song had been pretty much ruined by the swirling wind outside, Momma had been prevented from humming along with the tune which was her customary practice. Instead, she had kept herself distracted by peeling a bowlful of russet potatoes for our supper on this bleak midwinter evening in late January of 1952.

By the time full darkness had settled in across the countryside, something had changed. What was it that sounded so different?

The windowpanes all continued to rattle and the house itself still seemed to strain to even remain upright. But the wind was different. It no longer carried the tenor of a high-pitched whine but had transformed into a roar, a loud noise coming off the mountains to the north and bearing down onto the flatland farms out near Penrose.

Then, rather abruptly, the roar completely tapered off, making the stillness palpable. Windows were no longer rattling. Wind could no longer be heard whistling around the eaves and rafters. Only the faintest barking by some faraway dogs broke the eerie silence outside.

A sense of astonishment had entered the house. But there was anticipation among the occupants as well. What would happen next? Would the wind return as quickly as it had disappeared? Would the silence outside prevail all through the night?

It was Daddy who solved the mystery of the new quietness outside. It was just before three-year-old Gloria, known as Little Sister to the family, and

Johnny, at four years of age, were sent off to bed, with Gladys and David soon to follow by crawling under heavy bed covers for the night, that the front door was cracked open just wide enough to allow the lamp light to reveal huge snowflakes falling all around on the tiny front porch. Everyone, including Momma, scurried over to get a first-hand peek at the descending snowfall before Daddy slammed the door closed again to shut out the bitter cold. He then let loose a shrill whistle as he headed over to the wood stove to lean over it and vigorously rub his hands together.

We four kids drifted off into deep sleep to the faint sounds coming from somewhere in the distance, slightly haunting yet somehow soothing sounds of barking dogs from that neighboring farm way down east from our place. And no doubt the dreams that swirled around in our heads as we slept through that stormy night were filled with beautiful images of a Colorado landscape being transformed into a winter wonderland of white.

By morning, we discovered that an unannounced visitor had ventured to our front porch sometime during the night. He had become disoriented in the snowstorm, apparently, and had been unable to even find his way back to his own home.

We found a beautiful collie, now lifeless, curled up right by the door opening with his coat dusted with snow. Little Sister and I cried when Daddy said he had frozen to death overnight out on our porch, that he was probably very close to freezing before he ever found the porch during the wee hours of the night. He told us that the poor dog was very likely already too far gone to whimper or scratch at the door to escape the storm.

Both Gladys and David trudged through the newly fallen snow up to the school bus stop with hearts that were heavy. Momma tried to console Little Sister, who couldn't seem to control her sobbing, and I was not doing all that well myself.

We were finally calmed, though, by the assurance that our frozen overnight guest had been allowed into Doggie Heaven. That understanding gained by two very impressionable young children somehow made what had happened to our overnight visitor seem okay after all.

2   TALES FROM THE BOTTOMLESS LAKES

The two families were becoming more than casual acquaintances following an initial encounter after the Easter Sunday service. Interestingly, they had discovered that they both lived in the very same neighborhood with only three houses separating them. That made for easy walks down to their front porch for Saturday evening visits after each family had finished supper and put away the clean dishes by stacking them up on the open shelves above the sink once again.

The Loudermans were an older couple with only one child, an eighteen-year-old son named Gerald who was away most of the time working on the natural gas rigs outside of Hobbs and sometimes across the state line in west Texas near Midland and Odessa. None of us had met Gerald yet. His father, Vance, was tremendously proud of his son and had painted a rather glowing picture of him, having described him as a physically fit young man well-suited for the rigorous work of a roustabout. But it was his mother who had really gone on and on about his wages, bragging that Gerald brought home "real good money" every single week. And in

Nora's view, that was exactly what he needed—a good-paying job with regular paychecks.

To the Johnson preschoolers, Little Sister and her brother, Johnny, this Gerald Louderman, the son, had already grown into a bigger-than-life hero that we both were eager to see.

A first sighting would finally occur several weeks later. It was Saturday morning when he pulled into his yard in a green pickup and smiled and waved to us as we stopped our play of squishing our toes in the mud at the street gutter and straightened up to stare after him as he headed to his front door. We giggled, then sheepishly returned his wave.

So, there he was! Our new hero had strolled into the house wearing jeans and scruffy work boots with a white T-shirt that had the sleeves rolled up above his biceps on very tanned arms. His blond hair was mostly covered by a bright red ballcap.

Later, after dark while sitting cross-legged around his front porch, Gerald poured out his charm by regaling my two sisters and my brother and myself with fascinating stories about little horned toads and tarantulas and coiled rattlesnakes that could sometimes be spotted around his work site. Still other stories were completely made-up tales that were certain to entertain his young admirers. One of our favorite stories that we had begged him to retell over successive Saturday visits down to his porch was the one about a huge jackrabbit being chased by an old coyote. He would always begin that fabulous story by asking,

"Hey, now, have you kids heard the one about that big Texas jackrabbit and that mangy old coyote?"

Our response was always the same,

"Oh, yes! Tell it again. Please, please, please! Tell it again!"

He would then ask us to gather around tightly, to scoot up a little closer to him so that the sounds he made with his mouth and his arm movements would be more dramatic.

"It all happened one day down in Texas. The sun was getting pretty low. It was time to quit work for the day. We were just about to climb down off the rig when we saw him. There he was, just sitting on his haunches out in the dirt in front of one of the trucks. We could hardly believe our eyes! He was probably the biggest jackrabbit any of us had ever seen before. But there was something really crazy about him. It was his ears! One ear stuck up out of his head for a bit more than a foot, but the other one was all droopy. It was folded over and covered his right eye.

Then suddenly that rabbit hopped under the truck to hide from a mangy coyote that had slid to a stop from a full run. He whirled around with bared teeth and started snarling at the rabbit. He sure wanted that big rabbit for his dinner! But just how could he snatch him up from under the work truck where he was hiding?

Then, before any of us could even blink an eye, we saw that big droopy-eared jackrabbit dart out from underneath that truck and hop over toward one of the long steel legs that held up our rig. Of course, that blasted old mongrel ran off after him, but that one-eared rabbit just kept on outsmarting him by hopping around and around the four legs of the big platform where we were standing to look down to watch the action going on below us. Sometimes our Mr. Rabbit would lead the chase by hopping in circles. And sometimes he would go around and around in a figure-eight pattern that just drove that coyote bananas!

Then the Texas jackrabbit hopped back over to the front of the work truck and just stopped right there. Yes, he just stopped! The hungry coyote was really confused now. Why would the jackrabbit that he had chased and chased for his special dinner just suddenly stop? But he *had* stopped.

By now he could almost taste that rabbit! Now was his chance to sink his teeth into it and drag it down to the gully across the way to start feasting on that juicy bunny rabbit.

But just as Mr. Mangy Mongrel was about to make his pounce, that jackrabbit did something nobody had ever seen before and probably never will see again. And I mean nobody—not that nasty coyote nor any of his relatives anywhere around in Texas or up in New Mexico.

This is what he did. He raised up his other ear, that droopy one, and started in flapping it. His normal-looking ear started flapping, too. The rabbit made a gigantic hop forward with the two ears flapping away just like the wings on a seagull and the Texas jackrabbit soared up, up and away! He was flying! We all watched what we could hardly believe. Yes! It was a flying Texas jackrabbit! He was flying off to outsmart a few more coyotes somewhere else!

We roustabouts stood on the rig's platform with our eyes totally popping out of our heads! And our mouths were gaping wide open, too! What had we just seen? We just could not believe our eyes! A flying jackrabbit!

And then we had a good laugh at that mangy old mongrel of a coyote. He yelped over and over and over again. It was so loud that it sounded almost like a scream. And the funniest part of all was that he was letting out his yelps while standing on his hind legs and pawing the thin air in the exact spot where his dinner had just up and flown away!"

Oh, how we Johnson kids, especially Little Sister, loved that particular story! She could sometimes be seen hopping and jumping all around the yard with her thin arms flapping in full flight, teasing an imaginary coyote to catch her if he could!

There were two tales that Gerald assured us had not just been conjured up out of the blue, though. They were absolutely true, even hauntingly so, and would forever be remembered by anyone who ever heard them. We were quite young and extremely impressionable, but true stories can linger on and on in memory for a lifetime.

Little Sister still recalls, to this day, the sad story of the love birds who made a deadly promise to be together forever and cemented that commitment by a suicide pact to drive right over the edge and plunge into Devil's Inkwell, one of the bottomless lakes out east of Roswell, New Mexico. Elaine had even left a note atop her dresser in her bedroom, also signed by her lover, telling the wide world of the plan to spend all of eternity with Thatcher, her sweetheart since their junior high school days.

Another dreadful story from the summer of 1951 involved a middle-aged man who had deliberately gone over the edge at one of the nine bottomless lakes in a shiny new Chrysler sedan that had been reported as stolen from a private driveway way up in Albuquerque. Witnesses were able to tell the responding sheriff that the man had stopped the car and stepped out to peer over the edge before hurrying back to the driver's seat and gunning the engine to hurl himself into the lake some 125 feet below. Who could ever forget that true story? And the grim tale was made even worse by the report that his body and the automobile itself had never been located for recovery. To many, many people, that was all the information they would ever need to prove that the nine little lakes out east of town really were bottomless!

3   A BORROWED GUITAR

Someone had already partially opened the small screenless window on the side of the travel trailer that sat behind the newly abandoned house facing North Missouri Avenue. The small trailer was now being used only for storage and was bulging with miscellaneous pots and pans and loosely folded blankets and pillows and other household goods that were stacked all the way up to the ceiling, all clearly visible from ground level while standing in the back yard. One item stood out from its wedged position up against the window frame and grabbed the immediate attention of all four young Johnson kids. A polished wooden child's guitar with all the strings intact was pleading to be liberated from a rather precarious perch just inside the half-open window.

The active planning for just such a rescue mission immediately got underway by first determining the rationalization for the task at hand. We agreed that most of the stuff was probably nothing but pure junk, anyway, so everything was up for grabs since nobody lived on the property anymore. Moreover, action was needed to prevent the beautiful brown guitar from shifting and falling out of the window where it would surely break apart when it hit the ground. Should that happen, or if an overnight rain should soak it, we would feel terribly responsible if we failed to take appropriate action while we could.

Now a tactical course had actually been set. Little Sister, being the youngest as a four-year-old and the lightest, would be hoisted up by Gladys onto David's shoulders while I steadied her legs as she reached up to dislodge the treasure and liberate it from the junk-filled trailer. The retrieval did require some effort since the window had to be slid the rest of the way open, but before too long the pretty guitar was handed down to Gladys and Little Sister was lowered to the ground.

The effort to acquire the musical instrument had been a joint one among the four of us, but Gladys quickly claimed full ownership. After the rest of us loudly protested by saying that the cute little guitar should at least be passed around and shared, she chirped, "Possession is nine tenths of the law!" Then she skipped away up the gravel street toward home. At nine years old, she was the senior among her siblings and obviously intended to hang onto whatever privileges came with her age. While Little Sister and I didn't understand anything about the legality of her stated claim over the new treasure, we definitely understood that she meant exactly what she'd said. It was pretty clear that the only one who would ever get to strum the guitar strings would be Gladys herself, since even our brother David had been excluded.

It has long been said that even the best laid plans can sometimes fall apart, and our escapade down to the vacant house began to unravel soon after we entered our own house with the bounty tucked under our big sister's arm.

Our eyes were glued to the little instrument, and we were impatiently waiting for the first sounds to come from the guitar, any sound at all that would make the new possession known to our parents. Finally, Gladys began. She plucked a single string, then a second one, followed by several all at once in a strumming fashion while the fingers on her left hand pretended to work the frets along the neck of the guitar. But it was not music she was playing with her unskilled fingers. Not really. To even call it music would have been an enormous stretch, since the sounds weren't notes but only noise. And extremely loud noise at that!

Momma was first to react to the strange sounds coming from out in the living room by rounding the corner from the kitchen, potato masher in hand, to stare at the source of such a loud racket. Her face had a deep scowl as she looked at each of us kids, but nothing was said. She seemed too puzzled to ask questions of anyone. Besides, the loudness of that guitar strumming would surely have drowned out any attempt at communication anyway.

"What kind of monkeyshines is this? What's going on in here?"

Daddy's booming questions immediately brought complete silence from the noise-making guitar. We all sheepishly stared back at him as he stood near the kitchen doorway with his eyes narrowly focused on the device being held by Gladys.

"It's a guitar," we all mumbled in unison. "I can

see that! Where did you get it?"

As the telling of our little adventure from down the street slowly unfolded, the expression on Daddy's face started to harden significantly. Now our feat turned into a terrible nightmare as we sensed the wrath of our father. We were in real trouble now, in very real danger of a round of whippings!

"Now you kids straighten up and fly right! Do you hear me?"

Daddy paused long enough for Gladys to squeeze out a meek two-word apology,

"We're sorry!"

"You will take that thing back to where you stole it from, and you will do it first thing in the morning. It was never yours to take in the first place. I will not suffer any thieves in this house. No, I will not!

Tomorrow morning! Do you understand?"

It was Little Sister who magically saved our hides! She calmly claimed that we had only borrowed the precious little guitar by stating,

"Daddy, we only borrowed it. We didn't steal it."

Since Little Sister, as the baby of the family, could do absolutely no wrong whatsoever in her father's eyes, we were suddenly rescued. And the young girl recognized her contribution. She must have, if the little pursed mouth and quick glances around at the rest of us revealed anything!

We were accompanied on our return trip down the street the next morning by Daddy, who explained that the folks in the little vacant house, the Bartlett family, had moved back to Oklahoma less than a week before but planned to come back to haul out the trailer home. We wondered how Daddy would have that information about plans for the travel trailer but, completely out of character for him, he actually conversed with us as we walked. We were told that Mr. Bartlett had worked at the tire shop over on Main, the place where Daddy had met him when looking for two retread tires that he needed to purchase for the pickup. And it was during that transaction that he learned from the tire man that his ailing parents back home in Sayre needed him to leave New Mexico and return to Oklahoma to care for them, since emphysema was threatening to hospitalize his father while a mild stroke had already changed everything for his mother.

We listened intently. Then we asked him why the Loudermans had up and moved away during the first week of June, knowing that Daddy would have that story down since we knew them from church and all the Saturday evening visits at their house. His answer seemed straightforward enough but still somewhat vague, simply stating that people can get a real urge to move when summer arrives. The Loudermans had been bitten by the proverbial moving bug and had headed off to the Carolinas, wherever that was.

Now a process for returning the "borrowed" guitar was duplicated in reverse. An air of guilt hung over us, however, so the replacement felt a bit sneaky. Was that why Daddy watched us from afar at the front edge of the lot to avoid implicating himself in the rather clandestine operation?

We made fast work of the repositioning of the little brown guitar. Relieved to be free from our theft, we hurried up the street toward home to catch up with our father who had already left the area and had almost reached our own yard.

Nothing more was ever said about our short-lived possession of that treasured little instrument, not among ourselves and never by our parents, either. What was mentioned over supper that very same evening, though, was the upcoming move that we were about to make out into the country west of town. We kids were completely blindsided by that new information. A move way out to the country? Why? Why must we leave our nice house right here in town, the place where our oldest sister Gwen, along with her husband, Joe, had recently visited after driving down in their shiny brown four-door Hudson? So, why must we leave the place where Little Sister and I had endless fun every day playing prisoners trapped behind the torn chain link fence up at the corner of the front yard under the big elm tree, the spot where we would call out for rescue from drivers passing by on College Boulevard?

No! We didn't want to leave! But Daddy abruptly ended that announcement by simply stating, more to our mother than to us kids, that the moving bug had bitten him as well. We could tell that Momma was not the least bit amused by this development but was clearly powerless to intervene in any way.

While sitting at the table next to the open kitchen window, we all noticed when the pickup parked right outside had started moving backwards. What was going on? Then the slight crawl picked up a little as the truck reached the slight downhill of the driveway. Daddy jumped up and exclaimed,

"Someone is stealing the Chevrolet!"

We all rushed out the front door to stop the theft. What we discovered, instead, was a pickup that had rolled across the street and had come to an abrupt stop when the bumper and tailgate hit the shrubbery hedge on the neighbor's property line.

Daddy climbed into the cab and started the engine and drove it right back up beside the house while Momma shooed us in to finish our supper.

"I left it in neutral earlier today when I parked it. I sure didn't leave it in neutral now, though!"

So, that was why it took off on its own!

We kids all giggled and even Momma smiled when Daddy said,

"I just told you all that we would be moving out. But I didn't mean we'd take off today while we're having our supper!"

4 THAT SKINNY GIRL

The bite that Daddy had received in early June of 1952 from the "moving bug" must have really been a severe one. Not only did it sting so deeply that we packed everything up the very next day to drive away from our house up on College Boulevard, but the long-term effect was apparently so everlasting that an entire series of moves from one place to another occurred over the course of considerably less than two years. To little children, these moves around to different places out in the country west of town really didn't matter all that much. Little Sister and I were too young for school, and Gladys and David simply caught the big yellow school bus from whatever country corner had a bus stop.

The first country dwelling that we moved to was nothing more than a plain cabin-like structure with two miniscule bedrooms, one essentially only a lean-to with an outside entrance, on a lot that sat right up next to the construction area where West Second Street was being widened into a four-lane expressway west of the town. Enormous yellow Caterpillar tractors were at work every workday until being shut down at closing time. Little Sister and I thoroughly enjoyed running around barefoot on the freshly turned and smoothly graded soil.

One of the long afternoon adventures we took with David along a newly graded portion of the highway project had turned up an unbelievable treasure: a nearly perfect one-dollar bill that had blown in and lodged against a sculptured bank of freshly turned soil. David had knelt to pick it up and then gushed with excitement at the unexpected find. Everyone marveled at the crispness and feel of the bill, with Little Sister exclaiming, "Wow! I've never seen real paper money before!" And as a matter of fact, the rest of us hadn't either!

Another memory from the five months living out at that highway cabin took place inside the lean-to bedroom where we Johnson kids all slept. We still fondly recall the distinct sound of the strong wind as it whistled around the rafters of the windowless room while Little Sister and I lay curled up on the bed staring at the wide unpainted pine boards that formed the wall that the bed was wedged against, all the while listening to our sister Gladys as she read wonderful stories from a school library book entitled Meadowbrook Girls in the Hills.

Suddenly, we moved again!

By the time Gladys and David had climbed off the school bus and completed the short walk out to the cabin, both the pickup and trailer were already loaded, and we were just standing around waiting for them to climb up into the back of the vehicle. Momma smiled as she informed her children that we would really like our new place that was less than a full mile way, further stating that we must respect Mr. Roberts, the landlord, and avoid going where we shouldn't while on what she called the ranch. Flush with expectation, Little Sister was the first one to speak. She declared, in an incredulous manner, that we were now "going to be living on a ranch!" The excitement was electric in the back of the pickup as we sat scrunched up against boxes of household goods, straining to see out between the canvas-covered pickup bed and the limited view between the bumper and the trailer in tow. We wanted to fully absorb the surroundings that led to our awaiting abode.

Momma had been right. What a wonderful place for kids to live! We immediately loved it, from the front gate that was permanently kept open at the entrance on through to the dirt yard past the large stock tank with a wooden windmill frame topped with fourteen steel blades in full view of the white farmhouse with its two stories. There was a small barn with a corral attached at one end that held two horses. Horses! So, it really was a little ranch!

There was no time for any serious exploring after we had all piled out from the back of the pickup, since everyone's help was required to unload and set up before stopping for supper. But Little Sister and I both knew that with the new day, with Gladys and David away at school, she and I would have an entire first day to find out all that we could about every square inch of that ranch. And even though we had slept quite comfortably in the furnished farmhouse, we still awoke rather early, filled with anticipation of the adventure that awaited us.

After our breakfast of Post Toasties corn flakes, we burst through the kitchen door and made a beeline out to the corral to stand with one foot up on the bottom rung of the wooden fence to gaze at the two beautiful horses, one a pinto and the other a dappled gray, as they, in turn, stood watching us. Eventually, they both started ambling over toward us, perhaps expecting a carrot or handful of dry oats or maybe just to satisfy their curiosity about the young children, the almost four-year-old Little Sister, and the close to five-year-old Johnny. But never having been so close to such large animals, we both backed away at their approach and chose to continue viewing them from a safer distance!

The little flock of Rhode Island Red chickens had no interest whatsoever in approaching us, instead quickly moving off toward the protection afforded by the henhouse at the back of their enclosed wire coop.

As we turned away from the chickens to continue our investigation, we noticed a horseman riding a light brown horse slowly approaching through the front gate. The rider, dressed pretty much like we expected a real cowboy to look with cowboy boots and a black cowboy hat, stopped at the stock tank in the middle of the yard so the horse could take a long drink of the cool water. Glancing over toward us, he called out,

"Are yer folks about the place somewheres?"

I whispered to Little Sister that it was probably Mr. Roberts himself before we went tearing off to the kitchen door to tell our parents that some cowboy who talked funny, like maybe he was from Texas or some other strange place, was outside on a big horse asking for them. And by the time Daddy and Momma reached the door, the man had already left the watering tank and was sitting astride the horse right up by the porch.

"Well, howdy! Ya'll must be the Johnson family. I just came over from my place back that-a-way." He threw a thumb to gesture off toward the west. "I just wanted to meet you folks to see if there's anything ya'll needed. My name is Wade Roberts."

"Well, everything seems to be okay, Mr. Roberts. That windmill really seems to be doing the job just fine. I *am* wondering, though, how to go about the rent. Will that foreman of yours be coming by to collect on the first of every month?"

"Yeah. That won't be no trouble. He comes right by here ever single day anyways to take care of them horses and chickens. Oh, and missus, do take all them eggs. Just go to the coop of a morning and gather them up."

Momma beamed a huge smile at him as a gesture of thanks, and Daddy verbally thanked him for his generosity.

"All right, then. Let Ben know if anything comes up that ya'll need." With that, he turned his horse and waved a goodbye.

Little Sister and I then walked over to the big stock tank to check where that horse had been drinking. And to our astonishment, we saw several goldfish swimming around in the tank above algae covered rocks of various sizes and near some tall aquatic plants. What a wonderful discovery we had made! A few weeks later, too, we discovered that the ice cap that had formed on the tank during a cold snap in late December had not caused the loss of any of the fish. When the ranch foreman broke the ice a couple of days later, we rushed out in our warmest coats to see if our sweet little pets were still alive. To our complete delight, we saw every one of them still slowly swimming around at the very bottom of the watering tank!

Then we up and moved away!

It was truly a sad day when Little Sister and I had to bid farewell to the two horses and our precious goldfish.

We Johnsons didn't stay at the newest place out on West McGaffey Street all that long, but it was now 1954 and I had just started the first grade of elementary school by that fall. Unbeknownst to all but Momma, our father had managed to obtain a lot out in the country west of town and he spent each weekday out on the property preparing it for his own homemade stick-built house. Eventually the whole family would join him on weekends, so we were all able to observe the modest one-room house rise from the dirt of the bare lot.

When the structure was finally completed and the hand-dug cistern was filled with drinking water, we closed up all housekeeping in town on McGaffey Street and, yet again, made Auto Route West our address to start a brand-new life out in what was essentially the "sticks" west of Roswell in a house that we didn't have to fork out any rent money for. While extremely primitive, with only dirt flooring, no electricity and no running water, it was ours.

It was there at our new place where we Johnson kids met the four Serrano girls, and one of them, Esmeralda, was approximately the same age as Little Sister and me and rode the school bus with us. We and almost everyone else, with the major exception of her mother, just called her LaLa. We would play with her outside her home rather than ours pretty much every day, weather permitting, and learned Spanish songs that she happily taught us to sing, whether they were appropriate or totally inappropriate, like that fun one about the Mexican wedding of the drunken roadrunner and the crazy magpie!

One Sunday afternoon while playing alone outside at our place we heard, completely out of nowhere, music and a baritone voice singing, "There will be peace in the valley for me." This was followed by a song about a church somewhere in the wildwood and still another one about being in a garden and having someone walking and talking alongside the singer. The music and singing continued for what must have been a full hour. Where in this world was it coming from? Little Sister and I were totally flabbergasted by this new development out by our house, even after Gladys and David identified the source of the music. They informed us that it was coming from the metal steeple that sat atop the front end of the small Missionary Baptist Church located due west of us almost a block away. But how? Supposedly there was a loudspeaker hidden inside the steeple. It seemed way too complicated and even impossible!

Multiple Sundays came and went before we two youngest children believed what was clearly true, that everyone living near the tiny church was being serenaded every Sunday afternoon by somebody named Tennessee Ernie Ford from a pre-recorded program being played for all to hear from the little Baptist church.

As summer turned to mid-July, we responded to an invitation that had been hand-delivered over to our house that described what was being billed as Vacation Bible School right there across from us. We attended daily for an entire week and learned interesting stories about Jesus and participated in coloring pictures of characters from the Bible who all wore long, flowing robes, both men and women alike. What we would forever remember, though, were cookies and ice-cold Kool Aide served twice each day, first with a sandwich and potato chips at lunch and again in the middle of the afternoon. We marveled at how genuinely sweet and kind all the adults were toward the gathered children, even to the obvious ragamuffin strays that Little Sister and I must have looked like!

There was a single unkindness, though, that Little Sister accidently overheard. It was nothing more than a statement from a girl that she didn't even know at all, a young seven-year-old Donna Bly who had commented to a couple of her acquaintances about "that skinny girl" with the curly ponytail.

As hurtful as that was, it was not the first time my sister had been referred to as being skinny. Daddy had said it a few times and had even tried to rectify the problem. He forced her to drink the entire one-inch-thick cap of heavy cream that topped each gallon of jarred raw milk that was brought to the house every Saturday morning by Bro. Haymans. This gesture was his contribution to the real need for the family to receive, free of charge, what the Reverend Mark D. Albertson from the church had already prescribed as "poundings" for the needy among the church membership.

Little Sister's forced ritual each Saturday morning around nine during that summer was difficult to watch. That awful cream, even though refreshingly cold, was hard to swallow and always threatened her with significant gagging. Despite the difficulty with the process, though, Daddy insisted he was only trying to "fatten up" his baby girl.

But Little Sister was not the only impossibly skinny Johnson child. A picture had been mailed to each family awarded a place at a table for their child at the annual Christmas Breakfast provided by the downtown Optimist Club. The photo we received revealed my own dreadfully meatless arm as I sat next to Little Sister at the holiday table and was photographed while reaching for my glass of milk.

Luckily, I managed to escape having to go through the heavy cream ritual every Saturday morning out at the house. I was so fortunate to not be Daddy's youngest baby!

One sweet treat always awaited Little Sister each Saturday afternoon to somewhat compensate for the awful heavy cream requirement each Saturday morning. We each were given a nickel to purchase a wax-paper-wrapped All-Day Sucker. The candy wouldn't literally last an entire day, of course, but the suckers, in either a raspberry or grape flavor, would at least give almost two or three hours of pure enjoyment. And it was sometimes possible to even win a free one if the wrapper had the hidden prize symbol printed inside.

"Hey, Little Sister. You won a free one! What flavor will you get for your second All-Day Sucker?"

"Oh, I did *not* win, either! Of course I didn't. You're just full of beans!"

"Well, you didn't even look at the wrapper, then. Here. Take time to really check it out this time!"

She spread out the now-crinkled wrapper that had enclosed her raspberry-flavored sucker, followed by a squeal of happiness,

"I did win! Yes, I did! I'll get a grape one now!"

There would be no saving the extra All-Day Sucker for enjoyment on another day. Oh, no! Little Sister was committed to finishing both candies before the sun could go down. She planned to just stand outside by the kitchen window in the morning and brush her teeth longer than usual with the Colgate Tooth Powder kept in the red and white tin that sat on the outdoor wooden shelf waiting for use each Sunday morning. And that should take care of any overindulgence from the afternoon before!

Besides, two All-Day Suckers in a single day would mean extra sugar to help fatten up the hopelessly skinny girl we all knew as Little Sister!

5   A FIERY OVEN AT DAYBREAK

Were we just dreaming? The extremely loud sirens were relentlessly disturbing the quiet countryside, and the piercing noise seemed close. But before long everyone knew that we were not dreaming. A very real situation was underway outside, maybe even taking place on our own property or at least very, very close by. There were never emergency sirens way out this far from town. Never. What in the world was going on?

Then we kids heard our Daddy's loud exclamation,

"Well, I'll be a monkey's uncle!"

We all slid out from under our sheets and hurried off into the kitchen to discover our parents already outside beyond the doorway staring at an inferno across the open desert three blocks due north of our place. Gladys, David, Johnny, and Little Sister shoved at each other to be the first one to squeeze through the door to gawk, with gaping mouths, at the unbelievable spectacle before us of the two-hundred-foot-long Mortenson chicken barn totally engulfed in flames!

One firetruck with swirling red lights had already pulled up to the scene and the siren on that rig was slowly winding down. But it looked like two more trucks were still approaching, so the wailing noise continued until they were all positioned and water cannons began spraying the flames. Some yelling among the firefighters could be heard despite the loud crackling and searing sounds coming off the wooden structure itself. And we were quite certain that we all heard the wild squawking from most of the seven hundred or so hens as they were being roasted alive.

The dawning of the new day was still probably a half-hour away, but no one noticed any darkness. The glow from the flames completely illuminated the area all around us due to our head-on view of the massive fire. By now Little Sister had perched herself up on the pale green butane tank for her front-row viewing position to watch the morning disaster playing out in front of her. The rest of us, also still in our pajamas, were milling around a bit without ever being able to drag our eyes away from the horrific inferno. Even Momma and Daddy had not yet ventured back inside the house to begin their morning coffee routine. They, too, were held spellbound by the terrible scene unfolding over at the Mortenson place.

We could hear the water as it hissed against the wooden framework of the barn. It seemed puzzling that the torrent of pumped water directed right at the flames appeared to be completely ineffective. That ineffectiveness was fully displayed minutes later when the entire shingled roof came crashing down along the full length of the barn. At this point the support beams just ignited anew, seemingly, and no amount of water pumped from the engines could extinguish the fully engulfed dry timbers that now burned just like torches. It was clearly a losing battle now.

As dawn slowly spread across the eastern sky, the flames had died down considerably and yielded to billowing clouds of black smoke that spread the stench of scorched feathers and charred poultry flesh on the swirling wind. And by the time the first rays of sunlight illuminated the area of the fire, it was dreadfully clear that there was nothing at all left of the structure except heaps of smoldering, blackened refuse from what had previously been an impressively large barn to house laying hens. The operation had been the envy of every other family that kept a few chickens in a little coop out in the yard. But envy aside, everyone around them felt tremendous sympathy for Claude and Angie Mortenson because of their great loss. How would they be able to withstand such an early morning blow? People all around shuddered to think how devasted they must feel.

No one in our family was allowed to venture over to the still-smoldering remains of what had been the immense barn, although we kids were itching to know if the church at the far western end of the same property that faced Brown Road, that tiny square house of worship that was pastored by a female Pentecostal preacher that we knew, had also been burned to the ground. Many other folks, no doubt, yearned to go and poke around out of sheer curiosity but not one vehicle appeared to venture that way throughout the day except for a police car and a single red vehicle that most likely belonged to the fire department. There seemed to be some unwritten prohibition against any private investigation.

Was it now a crime scene? If not, why would a black and white police sedan be parked near the ruins for much of the day?

After the Saturday night routine of tub bathing by each child, we had again donned our pajamas and gathered around at our respective kitchen table chairs where we kneeled for the evening prayers before bed. This ritual was just that, a ritualistic approach to speaking to God at the end of each day by offering the very same prayer as always, starting with the oldest, Gladys, all the way down to the youngest, Little Sister. All four of us, taking turns, said the exact same prayer that went,

"NOW I LAY ME DOWN TO SLEEP,

I PRAY THE LORD MY SOUL TO KEEP, IF I SHOULD

DIE BEFORE I WAKE,

I PRAY THE LORD MY SOUL TO TAKE. AMEN."

Curiously, Momma would never pray out loud, but Daddy always started each session with whatever thoughts were at the forefront of his mind. And this Saturday night of the barn inferno, he paraphrased parts of Psalms 21 and 52 by declaring,

"They shall be plucked out of their dwelling place and be rooted out of the land of the living.

They shall be made as a fiery oven and the fire shall devour them."

Even Little Sister knew better than that! He could not be referring to those burned-up chickens. No! Each of us fully knew all about his penchant for spiritualizing any and every single thing, and this was a perfect example of that practice.

By the school bus ride home on Monday, the buzz had circulated that the tragic fire that caused the loss of more than seven hundred and thirty hens was indeed due to suspected arson. Rumor had it that a certain individual had already been arrested sometime on Sunday afternoon and booked as a prime suspect for deliberately setting the barn on fire by sloshing gasoline on the perimeter of the structure sometime during the wee morning hours of the Saturday blaze. That suspect had a name. It was Ray Rideman.

Everyone on the school bus knew Ray. He was only an occasional rider, climbing aboard if he chose to attend classes, which was quite seldom. He was older than other students in the school since he had been held back a couple of years for failing grades. Everyone, even those of us too young to comprehend any of it, certainly knew that he had already been accused of doing something terribly hurtful to a little girl from up north of the highway close to where he lived with his alcoholic parents. And everyone had heard by now that he had just been fired from his job at the Mortenson's chicken farm on Friday due to excessive absenteeism.

Oh, yes! Ray Rideman was undoubtedly guilty of that hideous crime against his former employers, an unforgivable act committed on that fateful pre-dawn Saturday morning. So, finally, that monster would surely be locked away in juvenile hall where he belonged!

Come to think of it all, perhaps those paraphrased verses from the Bible that Daddy had been tossing around during Saturday night prayers had found real lodging after all. Perhaps a fiery oven really did await our young arsonist!

We were almost there. The route up to Bartlesville had used up two whole days, but the Ozarks were just a few miles ahead. And then it happened! We children in the pickup bed heard the loud crack as the trailer tongue snapped while driving through a significant dip on the two-lane Oklahoma highway at a speed that proved to be just a bit too fast. And Daddy had probably heard the audible break in the wooden trailer tongue as well, plus he must have felt the dragging of the towed trailer as it scraped along on the blacktop.

As luck would have it, a wide and long spot to pull off beside the road was in the immediate vicinity albeit over on the other side of the roadway. But with no real choice in the matter, Daddy crossed over the center line to park the crippled outfit as far away from the highway as possible.

"Well, drat it! There goes another two days, maybe even three days. It will take time to get this fixed!"

Of course, every one of us had to stand around to survey the wreckage, but we kids soon tired of the inspection and took off to view a fast east-flowing river with water that was a deep green color from the reflection of the mixed hardwoods marching right down a hillside to the edge on the opposite side. Gladys had seated herself near the riverbank and had a faraway look as she followed the moving water to where it took a slight bend to the right. But David and I and Little Sister all stood right up at the edge and were totally transfixed while staring at the deep water, a spell soon broken, though, when Gladys called out,

"I knew it! I knew I saw something moving down in that water! Look over there where the sunlight is hitting the bottom. See it? Right there it is! See that green turtle swimming along?"

And there it was in full view! The turtle appeared to be in no hurry as it swam along near the bottom in slow motion in the same direction as the current. By the time it had moved out of the sunlit area at the bottom, it disappeared from discernable view down in the murkiness of the deep green of the river water in shadow. Then another one appeared in the sunlit water! It was a bit smaller and seemed to be in a much bigger hurry. Was it chasing after the first one? We remained at the edge of the river for a long time in hopes of seeing the turtles once again, but finally moved away after about an hour had passed. Besides, the sun was hot, and it was extremely humid, so seeking shade became a new priority.

When we walked back over to the broken-down rig, we all noticed that Daddy was nowhere to be found and were told that he had taken off in search of some sort of river crossing, since a new timber from over on the other side would be necessary to replace the trailer tongue. Momma even lamented that such a journey might take up much of the day. And she was worried about how he would manage to drag the new timber all the way back by himself. She said he had shouldered a long length of rope and his bow saw in anticipation of getting the job accomplished, though.

Gladys decided it was time to find a cool, shady spot somewhere and delve into a good book, while David, Little Sister and I took off to explore the rest of the large roadside pull off. There wasn't much to see, really, since the river was the main draw. All we found was a large broken down cardboard box and two discarded Coors beer cans. Someone decided to write a warning with a crayon on the folded-out cardboard that was then attached to a couple of sturdy branches and angled toward the highway for drivers to see. The message, dictated by Little Sister, was straightforward and stated in capital letters,

"BEER MAKES YOU DRUNK. DON'T DRINK IT."

The new trailer tongue fashioned from a green tree trunk required two whole days to complete before we were finally rolling down the highway again. We visited the river several additional times during the delay in a failed attempt to spot turtles once again. Something was spotted, though, and it thoroughly scared us. After lifting a medium-sized boulder by the sloping riverbank to investigate why there was a narrow-burrowed trail leading to a little entrance under it, we screamed and let the rock crash back down at the sight of a small color-banded snake that was just lying there sleeping. We would never really know if it was a true coral snake, but that full knowledge did not matter to us at all. We ran far away from that spot with a firm determination to avoid the area forevermore!

After the delay of several days out beside the river, groceries were very low. So, at another roadside pull off, this one an intentional rest stop furnished with concrete picnic tables on either side of the highway, Daddy unhitched the trailer with its new trailer tongue and he and Momma drove off to find a town with a grocery store. We were hungry and waited at the table hoping some sort of food would be brought back soon.

It was Little Sister's idea! How dare she even do it? But it happened right under our noses. It mortified both Gladys and David so much that they quickly disappeared behind the trailer as soon as the man approached. He was a telephone lineman, one of the four sitting at one of the picnic tables directly across the highway as they took their lunch break.

"I'm so hungry! Can you spare something to eat?"

Even though I remained seated at the table, I, too, was aghast at the brashness of Little Sister when she had hollered to the men across the road. After a pause, she had repeated herself, this time with a louder voice. Without question, each of the four linemen had heard her, since they were all looking our way. Then it unfolded! One of the guys rose from his table with something in both hands. After looking both ways, he crossed the highway and, with a big smile, handed Little Sister half of a wax paper-wrapped sandwich, a bright red apple and a small yellow one, plus a large chocolate brownie.

She did manage to utter a barely audible, "Thank you," to which the man simply smiled again and turned to rejoin his coworkers who were already climbing into the company truck to leave.

Gladys was so furious! She made both of us at the table promise to not tell Momma and Daddy what had just happened, and she demanded that we get rid of the apple cores and the piece of wax paper in such a way that they could not be discovered anywhere.

It took a great deal of coaxing for her to accept her quarter of the brownie, but David was much easier to persuade. He gathered up his corner piece and thoroughly examined it as if it were a piece of fine artwork before even taking the first bite!

It was the typical Sunday night altar call. Nothing was unusual about an altar call, since an invitation always concluded every message that Bro. Styles ever preached. One man had responded and was kneeling at the old wooden altar on the right—the one designated for the men—up in front near the pulpit. What *was* unusual, though, was what had been placed on the altar out in front of him. A bent flask with an almost-full whisky bottle protruding from it and a pack of Pall Mall cigarettes had been spread before his folded hands.

It was also somewhat unusual how the preacher had stood over the kneeling man with one of his hands resting atop the man's balding head and the other raised heavenward. His prayer was loud, so loud that everyone seated anywhere in any of the pews could have heard his words as he repeatedly called out to the Lord to rebuke the devil in Jesus' name. Three other churchmen, probably deacons, had also stood nearby and offered less aggressive and certainly quieter prayers. After the preacher had finally toned down his volume considerably, another voice suddenly rang out from yet another man who had walked up just behind the penitent individual and shouted, at the top of his lungs,

"BOOT DAT DIVVER IN JIVVER NAME! BOOT DAT DIVVER IN JIVVER NAME! O, BOOT DAT DIVVER IN JIVVER NAME!"

Stifled giggles had broken out among the young children and even among some teenagers of the church at this outburst. Everyone who attended that church knew, of course, that this man's heart was in the right place in his endeavor to help in the rebuking of Satan, but everybody also knew that Jameson, poor ole Mr. Jameson, was an individual with a seriously debilitating speech impediment. The congregants, including most of the children and all the young people, felt tremendous pity for him. Although an occasional teenaged bully would decide to harass him, usually behind his back but sometimes even directly to his face, he was largely left alone and was generously smiled at instead of engaged by any impossible conversation. He had been a member for several years and had always faithfully tithed every Sunday on his meager Social Security wages, as had his protective wife, Ruby. So, yes, Jameson's heart was absolutely golden!

The weather was perfect by the first week in May. Flowers were in bloom in most everyone's yard, and the trees had already leafed out all around. The walk home from school no longer required a jacket or sweater now that temperatures hovered in the mid-seventies. And this Friday walk was only different in one major regard. My friend Randy had rushed up to me while on the schoolyard before Little Sister had left her classroom to join me on our walk home. Randy had sneaked a paper bag under my arm and breathlessly stated that it was a full carton of cigarettes that he had pilfered from the little market where we would always purchase Hollywood candy bars, those dark chocolate ones with black walnut studded nougat inside. Another carton was stashed between his textbooks under his left arm. He said to be sure and let him know on Monday whether I liked menthol cigarettes as he thrust three little packets of matches into my hand before running off in the opposite direction.

Contraband! And stolen contraband at that! But before I could begin to comprehend what had just happened, let alone assign any moral implications to it, Little Sister appeared at my side and the trek home had begun.

We had already made our way all the way down the steep hill and had passed by the little service garage where we always bought the coal oil for our house lamps. It was on this customary zig-zagging route home that Little Sister noticed the package under my arm and wanted to know what I had.

"Oh, it's nothing," I fibbed.

"I can see that it *is* something. What do you have there, Johnny?"

"Well, all right then, Little Miss Nosy. If you must know, follow me."

I diverted off to the right and took a little path that led straight down to the live creek, stopping at a high creekbank to check if she had followed. And, sure enough, there she stood with her shoes now as muddy as mine. She then reached for the sack to snatch it away from me, so I just blurted out the information,

"It's a full carton of cigarettes, all right? They are supposed to be menthol cigarettes. So, let's open this up and check it out."

Since Little Sister would usually do anything that I did, I had no qualms about sharing the contraband secret. She would willingly be in on it, too, exactly like that single time many years earlier when I had introduced her to the wonderful smell of gasoline from the spout of the portable gas can and then talked her into a very long walk over into Dogtown, a disappearance of sorts that had worried Daddy so gravely that he had to go searching for us. We were eventually located inside the darkened and dingy shack of a bedraggled old man who called himself Steadman, a stranger who had invited us in for nothing more than idle conversation.

Little Sister and I had some real history together! So, there were no concerns whatsoever about our little cigarette secret.

The carton of Kool Filter Kings slipped right out of the paper sack and almost landed in the wet mud on the ground. I hurriedly opened one end of the carton, pulled out a pack, and relished the feel of the unopened pack in my hand. I couldn't wait to light one up, so, fishing around in the pocket of my trousers to locate a book of matches, I lit one and began to smoke my very first cigarette, somehow knowing not to inhale any of the smoke, though.

Little Sister then jumped right in and had me light one for her. She had only recently turned ten and I eleven, so we were thrilling to once again sowing a few wild oats together!

We remained down at the creekbank for the better part of an hour, lighting one cigarette after another and tossing the still lit but half-finished ones down into the flowing creek water that, within one block, would flow right past our own house. Even though neither of us was actually inhaling even a whisp of the menthol tobacco smoke, we nevertheless had begun to feel a little tinge of queasiness, so it was time to stop our little sinful adventure and head on home. After I located a safe spot for stashing the remaining carton of Kool cigarettes and matches, we climbed back up to street level and walked on home to enter through the rear kitchen door.

We did spend time to plan our strategy should our muddy shoes come into question or if we faced a challenge for arriving home later than usual. And we reminisced about that day as preschoolers out at that little ranch when I had discovered a nearly empty flask of rye whiskey in the outhouse, and we had both wrinkled our noses at the pungent smell and puckered up from the stinging sensation when barely even touching the bottle to our lips. We had promised each other that we would keep that little escapade a secret forever, just exactly the way we fully intended to keep this little caper down by the creekbank hidden forever!

Just how incredibly naïve can two youngsters be, anyway? We were clueless about the horrendous stench of stale cigarette smoke which was all over our clothing and reeking on our breath as well.

Neither of us was hungry for supper. No! We were positively queasy instead, so we headed straight through the kitchen where our parents were still seated at the supper table and where Little Sister pronounced that we were not hungry at all as we passed by. We had scarcely made it into the front room before we heard loud scraping of a kitchen chair against the floor and the heavy, rapid steps of Daddy as he burst through the doorway. We had managed to sit down on the couch, but our faces must have told an obvious tale on us. He walked over and commanded that we stand up. He then grabbed both of us by our skinny arms and yanked us up to his face level and thundered,

"Have you two kids been smoking?" "No, Daddy!

No, we haven't!"

He held us there for what seemed like an eternity as he looked first at one then the other of us, back and forth, without saying anything more. We were certain our lives were in mortal danger, hanging in the balance by a single thread. Then a real miracle occurred right before our terrified faces! We saw something in his eyes that was so special, a look of absolute compassion for his little children who were blatantly lying to him. He showed a father's mercy!

By then Momma had entered the room to witness our being let back down with Daddy moving back into the kitchen. She told us to quickly change our clothes and brush our teeth, then come and get some supper if we got hungry.

I was grateful that I had been spared from being thrashed to within an inch of my life. That reprieve was because the whole escapade was in concert with Little Sister, the one that Daddy could never bring himself to harm. So, in this instance, my life had indeed been saved by Little Sister!

7   ORANGE CREAMSICLES

His name was Freddie, but to all the neighborhood children he was just called Mr. Ice Cream Man. He lived in a small pale-yellow trailer located just off the alley and directly across from us at 3501 West Pierce in Phoenix. He was a recent widower, and his life seemed completely devoted to bringing joy through ice cream sales to all who would run out in response to the sound of the thumb-operated bell attached to the right handlebar of his three-wheeled motorcycle-powered ice cream cart. He carried various flavors of the frozen treat, but the very best choice he stocked just had to be those wonderful orange creamsicle ice cream bars that came on a stick, priced at ten cents apiece. Less expensive ice cream cones were available down at the Thrifty Drug Store for only five cents for each scoop, but it was a long, hot walk to get all the way down to the corner of McDowell Road and back.

We could always see when he was at home from our vantage point at the house. He didn't seem to mind at all having to come outside or rise from his shady spot under the patio cover to accommodate us on those occasions when we were able to piece together the two nickels necessary to purchase an orange creamsicle. He seemed to enjoy each visit by exclaiming,

"Well, hello my two teenaged friends! How are you doing on this hot day? Do you two need something to cool off with?"

And Little Sister's response, at thirteen years-of-age, was always the very same,

"You know exactly which ice cream Johnny and I need to handle this awful heat! You haven't run out of those, have you?"

We usually joined him under the awning while we slowly savored our treats. The conversation was mostly one-sided as he shared stories of his late wife Evelyn from the many years they had made Arizona their home. After the passing of his wife, a nursing supervisor at the largest hospital in all the city, Freddie had dramatically downsized into his modest yet comfortable trailer. With no children of his own, "adopting" the neighborhood kids had just come naturally.

Occasionally we had stories of our own to tell, like the terrifying one that Daddy had said he'd never expect to see again in a "month of Sundays." The story was about that thick rattlesnake we found the previous Saturday coiled up under the kitchen table in our rental house that belonged to old Mr. Rotmanski who ran the dilapidated used furniture store at the front of our lot facing busy 35th Avenue.

Freddie mentioned that he had wondered what all the Johnson kids were doing for so long out on the dirt driveway on that day. He had noticed that we were continuously poking at something with long sticks but had been unable to guess what we were focused on unless maybe it was a tarantula. But after he heard about the headless but still writhing rattlesnake, he leaned forward to tell another tale about a diamondback that had recently terrorized him, too, when he spotted it slithering along in a southernly direction down the alley. He just sat very still and waited. And he was thrilled when a big utility truck came along and flattened the viper right there in the middle of the alleyway!

He then lowered his voice and said something that really frightened us,

"I wouldn't be surprised at all if a rattlesnake den is located under that big pile of scrap lumber right over there in your back yard."

What a memory that dire warning triggered in us! Little Sister then proceeded to tell the whole story from years earlier when our New Mexico neighbors out in the country, the Metlows, had discovered a rattlesnake den under the crawl space of their own house. Unfortunately, that discovery had come at great personal loss. Their twin five-year-old sons, Ronny and Donny, had been exploring under the house and had been bitten repeatedly by the baby rattlers from the pit. One boy lost both of his legs while the other one suffered the loss of just one leg from the poisonous venom they received before they could manage to crawl back out and scream to their mother for help.

It was a Wednesday just before noon by the time Little Sister and I had finally managed to cobble together the two dimes needed for our ice cream. We hurried across the street to secure our orange creamsicles before Freddie could take off on the motorcycle to start his three-hour afternoon run to all the places his normal route would take him.

We made it with what we guessed was about five minutes to spare. Soon that delicious frozen treat would start cooling us down! But where was the peddler? He wasn't seated in his chair under the patio cover and no response was given when we knocked on the trailer door. His motorcycle cart was still in the usual spot, so we figured he must be running late. We plopped down in the shade to just wait for him to come out, since it was almost time for him to leave on his neighborhood rounds.

How much time had passed, anyway? I rose to knock on his door again, and did so considerably louder than before, but still with no response. By the time we gave up completely and went back home empty-handed we had determined that he had maybe walked somewhere or been picked up by friends. But those dimes were burning holes in our pockets, so we kept an eye on that motorcycle throughout the remainder of the hot afternoon.

We tried to buy our ice cream again on Friday but were not able to see him. It wasn't until Saturday in the late afternoon when we noticed activity at his place, but it was in the form of a squad car from the Phoenix Police Department. Within less than an hour we witnessed a van with Maricopa County Medical Examiner markings on the side. It backed right up to the trailer. Eventually a maroon-draped stretcher was rolled out of Freddie's trailer home and loaded up to be driven away.

Momma figured out what might have happened. She told us that someone had probably called in a welfare check on the man and the police official found that he had expired inside his trailer home.

For Little Sister and me, personally, and certainly for all the others who responded to his daily ice cream bell, it was extremely sad to know that our Mr. Ice Cream Man was no more.

8   BROWNED BISCUITS

"I was in a rather bad mood all day."

The new journal entry had been written in haste late that afternoon long after the noontime meal had wrapped up. The entry was intended to forever cement the offensive event. The journal itself was still practically new in its brilliant yellow binding with some penciled-in remarks here and there that were meant to inaugurate the cherished gift she had received at Christmastime just short of three months earlier.

Was she planning to blame someone other than herself? A plot was already developing to find a way to do just that. But it wasn't as if she could disagree. Not really. After all, anybody in her right mind could clearly see that the assault directed at her brother had been offered straight from the cuff without a shred of forethought. Instead, she had allowed the hurtful statements to flow as if they were somehow valid rather than just so incredibly asinine and so far off base that they deserved no more than a hearty laugh.

By now it was too late for any meaningful recovery. She was way too angry now to even try to come around to any reasonableness, any correction to what she had already said. Any awkward attempt at some feeble apology would not be forthcoming. There could be no retreat now. And absolutely no surrender.

The words between the two teenaged siblings had been caustic, certainly, but never intended to last into all eternity by way of some journal entry. Why couldn't they have been left in the dirt yard outside where they had been spoken? Why couldn't they have just been set loose like all the tumbleweeds blowing across the countryside?

Instead, what *did* get set loose was much like a desert dust devil, with angry words and outlandish accusations swirling around and around with ever increasing intensity and hurtfulness.

Without question, every bit of it would have been better left unsaid.

And where would one look for a speech filtering protocol for the Johnson family to use, anyway? Unfortunately, criterion for maintaining decorum within the family unit and beyond did not exist. It never had, which left every unbridled tongue with complete freedom to spew vile damage anywhere, anytime.

What *had* always existed, however, was an iron-clad prohibition against ever using any profanity whatsoever. Raw slander, untruths and hideous accusations coming straight out of a pig's wallow were very treacherous but were still more or less acceptable in general.

But inescapable hellfire awaited anyone who ever swore at another person or ever cursed about any difficult situation that arose, for that matter. We Johnson kids had been thoroughly indoctrinated with that clear understanding, truly believing that hellish punishment was unlikely to be meted out while languishing in some temporary waystation down in Purgatory. Rather, full punishment would come from an eventual shove that would result in a headlong plunge down into the hottest flames reserved for such sinners.

No cursing was ever uttered, not even underneath the breath. But a devilish speaking tone, coupled with hateful statements or actions, were always another matter altogether. Any such behavior was basically unpunishable. How very convenient!

"Johnny started it all by saying that I was stupid or something of the sort. So, is he turning out to be just like Daddy? It sure feels that way today. Daddy is always putting someone else up higher than me and running me down."

The whole thing started over nothing more than homemade biscuits. Little Sister had pulled them out of the oven and set the hot pan on the waiting potholder right next to the heaping plate of crisply fried cornmeal mush patties. But something was off. Way off. They smelled like biscuits. But aside from the evenly browned tops, they really didn't look much like biscuits at all. What was wrong? They were resting there in the pan, all eight of them, but were as flat as little pancakes. Not even one of them had risen as expected. After gingerly poking at a couple of the oven-hot discs with a forefinger, I exclaimed, "These are your biscuits? They're hard as rocks!"

If looks could have killed, I was very soon to be a dead brother! Little Sister was taking turns glaring at me and then glancing at the unrisen circles of baked dough that were intended to be delicious biscuits for our meal. But, since I would be a dead man soon enough anyway, I decided to forge right ahead with my ridicule of her efforts,

"Biscuits, you say? These perfectly sized hockey pucks are supposed to be biscuits? Well now, let's just see. I'll bet that Shadrach will enjoy gnawing on them. At least they won't be a complete waste, right? Wait! Hold on just a minute here. I've got it! We can use them for golf balls! We really do need something better than those little rocks we've had to use out front on our miniature golf course. I do think these will probably just skip right along. Plus, they have brown tops, so they'll be a bit easier to see on the dirt. Oh, yes! These so-called biscuits of yours will be just perfect!"

There was real hurt in her voice as her words were spoken, words that were only meant to serve as an explanation for the dismal baking failure,

"I must have forgotten to put in the baking powder. I know I did have the can of Clabber Girl powder sitting out on the table. Maybe they needed some baking soda, too. I'm just not sure."

It was now time to immediately pounce on Little Sister,

"Good grief! Just how stupid can you get, anyway? You forgot the baking powder?"

"Stupid, huh? Is that what you really think about me? Well, I'd like to see you make some biscuits, Mr. Smarty Pants!"

The meal was now over. I had been filled by the crispy cornmeal mush patties and was standing around outside in the early afternoon sun on this windy Saturday during the first week of March. Little Sister and I were alone at the house, since Momma and Daddy had driven out to spend the week in Phoenix and had taken young six-year-old Geneva with them.

My sister was in charge of each breakfast, dinner, and supper and had shown seriousness in taking on that big responsibility. The last thing this sibling of mine, younger by eleven months, deserved was to be mocked and deliberately embarrassed over her meal preparation. But that's exactly what I had done, shamelessly. Now I had determined to stop the playful yet very hurtful banter about all those failed biscuits and just let it all die down.

My attention was directed over to the windblown clothesline where shirts and cotton dresses and dingy white kitchen towels were angrily flapping in the brisk wind. I had turned back toward the house to go in for the clothes basket, since everything on that clothesline was certainly already dry. Each item was even threatening to break loose from the straight clothespins, the type without springs, that anchored them precariously to the wire line. From the way things appeared it wouldn't be too much longer before something, probably several things, · managed to pop free from the wooden fasteners and sail away to parts unknown before eventually snagging on some dusty sage brush or maybe get attached to a tumbleweed as it lumbered by.

Just then the side door opened and out came Little Sister. The hard look in her eyes made it clear that the failed attempt at baking was not yet resolved between the two of us, and probably far from it. I halted my progress toward the door as I heard the first volley shouted at me,

"Johnny, you're exactly like Daddy! You guys are just alike, like two peas out of the very same pod. It's way past time that I finally told you so, too!"

Her rapid steps toward me had abruptly stopped, leaving only a foot of shouting distance between us. And the shouting continued, carried downwind for everyone even a full quarter mile away to hear,

"What gives you and Daddy the right to run people down? Huh? And what gives you any right, Johnny, to just step in and take over and act so much like Daddy while he's out in Arizona? What right, I ask you? I demand an answer!"

Now Little Sister had gone too far—way too far! It was exactly what she had intended. She already knew that one of the last things this sixteen-year-old guy would ever want to hear was a comparison to our father. She knew that I would wither under any such direct comparison to Daddy. She also knew exactly how to dig and twist any similarities to deliberately hurt me. But to say that I was just like Daddy was meant to send me over the edge, and it had. And she knew it had. That knowledge seemed thoroughly delightful as reflected in her eyes which were gleaming as she watched me try to find an appropriate response.

I turned away in disgust but quickly whirled back around to coldly inform her that she was Momma all over again,

"You know, you've always been just like Momma, haven't you? Oh yes, Gloria, you are exactly like Momma! You even look like her!"

She was now on the verge of crying. It had all been too much for her, too. But she managed to throw out one last shot as she turned away to run back inside the house,

"I hate you! I hate you! Why don't you just go jump in a lake, okay? You go ahead and drown, too, for all I care! Oh, how I hate you!"

By five o'clock in the evening I had already been sitting in the nearly worn out but still comfortable brown overstuffed chair by the window in the living room for a couple of hours. I was preoccupied with leafing through all pages of the Spring & Summer mail order catalog from Montgomery Ward that had only recently been mailed out to Auto Route West and deposited in our rural mailbox up at the highway. The huge book of dreams, one thousand pages thick, was exactly that. It provided a dream-filled escape into the world of prosperous living, a prosperity already enjoyed by so many in America by the 1960s.

But the Johnson family could only imagine actually ordering anything from the offerings presented in full color. The catalog fueled the fantasies of those of us who did look through each seasonal mailing. But *every* member of the family did gain eventual value from each page, since all outdated issues of the catalog served a quite necessary purpose after finding lodging on a shelf inside the tiny place at the very back of the property at the end of a certain well-worn path.

"Supper's ready and on the table now. Come and get it."

"Nah, I'm not hungry."

Actual hunger was causing periodic growls in my stomach, and I would gladly consume anything at all that Little Sister had prepared, but there would not be any admission of that need. Even though I had managed to settle down almost completely from the anger that had dominated the immediate period after our fight, lingering resentment toward my sister remained. It would take a bit more time to free myself from that poisonous sense of having been so mercilessly labeled as a pea from the very same pod as my Daddy, to have been told that I, at only sixteen-years-old, was already just like him.

The characterization had cut me deeply. And while I recognized that I, in turn, had cruelly labeled her as stupid, a consignment completely undeserved, I nevertheless retained my own feelings of damage from that rather acerbic tongue-lashing from her following the noontime debacle over failed brown biscuits. So, there would not be any admission of suppertime hunger. No siree!

"But I warmed up one of the big cans of beef and gravy. And I boiled some potatoes that I mashed up with lots of butter and salt and pepper. Plus, there's batter bread with sugar on top, too."

Oh, dear! Now she had me. There was no resisting that wonderful shredded beef and gravy, a special meal made from the supply of surplus commodity foods that were picked up downtown at City Hall every month. But as I rose out of the easy chair and headed out to the kitchen, my mind flashed to the day of the week. It was a Saturday. Momma would only serve the large can of beef and brown gravy for our dinner meal after church every Sunday, so this supper, on Saturday evening, was out of order.

That did not matter to Little Sister. She oversaw preparations for every meal for a full week and she could make whatever choices she pleased. And as for me, I was delighted to get this particular meal a full day early!

As I took my place at the supper table, I noticed just a hint of a sheepish grin cross Little Sister's face. That smile caused my mind to flash back to something else—a distant memory of one special time, two years earlier, when the dinner table had been set with something that was also completely out of the ordinary.

The remembrance had been of one Sunday dinner when Momma had prepared the same beef and gravy with mashed potatoes, canned sweet peas, a lettuce and tomato salad smothered in Miracle Whip, and a dessert she had never served before. It was a homemade crushed pineapple double-crust pie! Daddy and we kids had returned from the drive into church for the morning service and detected the unbelievable aroma of the pie as we walked into the kitchen at exactly twelve-thirty. No doubt we looked in total amazement at Momma, who just returned our gazes with a big, toothy grin without commenting with even a single word.

What? A pineapple pie with loads of white sugar baked right onto the top crust! All of us wondered if the making of this dessert was a direct result of having the pure luxury of the morning off as she had stayed at home rather than ride along in the pickup into church.

Yes, that remembrance did seem comparable to this Saturday evening supper placed on the table before us. This meal was special. Had she learned this behavior from our Momma? And that trace of a smile had significance, didn't it?

Neither of us would ever utter an apology to each other. But the offending words were past us now, and we enjoyed a delicious supper together as if nothing had happened between us at noontime.

9 ONE SPECTACULAR CONVERTIBLE

Little Sister had certainly never intended to fall head over heels in love with him!

Every high school girl in the youth group down at the church was attracted to the young man. How could they help it? They simply couldn't. After all, they saw him as a good-looking guy with money—at least enough money to dress very well and sport around in his brilliant red 1959 Ford Galaxie 500 convertible. What girl anywhere didn't fantasize about riding shotgun or, even better, snuggled up against him as he drove up and then down again on Main Street in Roswell, first up to Greer's, that drive-in hamburger joint at the top of the hill for a fifteen-cent burger and ten-cents worth of fries, and then down to Wylie's at the Y at the south end of town for a twenty-five cent vanilla milkshake? Even the carhops at both locations swooned over the car and flirted with him as much as possible despite his date sitting right beside him. And what sheer ecstasy to be seen in that top-down car at the open-air drive-in picture show (for those who would dare to participate in that sinful pleasure) to catch the screening of The Sound of Music!

One of the very best things about Bob Stevens was that he was an airman stationed down at Walker Air Force Base just a few miles outside of town. An airman! Being able to date an actual airman was the equivalent of being the girlfriend of one of the varsity football jocks, that exclusive club afforded only to the cheerleaders.

But even better than being an airman, he was a church-going young man—and a Pentecostal one at that! His job on base was to work the day shift without any duty requirement on weekends. This sweet arrangement allowed attendance at every Sunday School hour and preaching service as well as for the return to 1212 North Washington Avenue at seven-thirty for each Sunday night service.

This airman was an unbelievable catch, and Little Sister, a junior in high school and now exclusively known as Gloria, had managed to snag him! She told me, her older brother, that it had been a very simple catch, one that was related to her flashing a beautiful smile at him that Sunday night in late April when he had turned to locate the source, two rows behind him, of the beautiful soprano notes he had heard during the congregational singing of the ballad-like hymn,

TELL ME THE STORY OF JESUS, WRITE ON MY

HEART EVERY WORD.

TELL ME THE STORY MOST PRECIOUS, SWEETEST

THAT EVER WAS HEARD.

Bob appeared very eager to meet her and made a beeline back to her row just as the service ended. Little Sister again smiled at him but blushed a little as she thanked him for the nice compliment on her singing voice. Her shyness was evident during the exchanging of names. And her face became quite flushed at his forthrightness in asking if he could drive her home from church in his car. Glancing around until she could catch my eye, she mouthed out the proposal from Bob and searched my face until I gave a nod of approval.

By the following Sunday he had sat with her during church and had accepted her invitation to come out to the house for Sunday dinner and to spend the afternoon until the evening service would take everyone back into town. Momma put on her best meal made from surplus commodity food, while Daddy sized him up a bit by asking him to say the blessing over the noontime meal. Apparently, he passed muster with his prayer, since Daddy made conversation by asking what his job entailed as an Air Force enlisted man. Little Sister, naturally, saw this as total acceptance of Bob, the young airman from Kansas. Her initial worry about obtaining her father's approval of her boyfriend had now come to an end.

But Little Sister had also worried about something else. She was very nervous about Bob's potential reaction to the long revival underway that meant nightly services for a projected three whole weeks with the possibility of the meetings being extended on a week-by-week basis. Would he tire of such a commitment to being in church night after night?

Or, alternately, would he be thrilled by the special singing and the fiery preaching from two traveling evangelists, Loretta and Lorraine Vinson, the twin sisters who sang and played accordions and took turns with the nightly preaching?

They also took turns driving their gorgeous orange DeSoto Fireflite Sportsman with those enormous tailfins! And what a fabulous package those two sweet ladies always presented when crossing the street after exiting their amazing hardtop coupe! Who could have really believed that a long revival meeting could be successfully conducted by such beautiful and elegantly dressed single women?

An invitation to "go steady" had been extended to my sister. That request from Bob had been readily accepted and was acted upon by weekend after weekend of sporting around in that spectacular red convertible with Little Sister's long brown hair flowing out behind her as the vehicle raced around the New Mexican desert near Roswell.

One Saturday had been spent out at Bottomless Lakes State Park driving from one sinkhole to the next before stopping at the largest body of water, Lea Lake, for fountain drinks and grilled cheese sandwiches from the concession window. Gloria delighted in telling Bob about the various legends attached to the lakes, like the one about a horse that had fallen into one of the deep lakes and had eventually resurfaced almost ninety miles away inside one of those water-filled areas at Carlsbad Caverns Park. That legend would always be so very spooky, she declared, even if someone believed the more plausible version of the old dead horse showing up in one of the other nearby sinkholes!

But she had saved the very best stories for last; she assured Bob that all the suicide plunges by automobile were completely true as documented by the Chaves County Sheriff's Department. And those stories, too, would always be spooky!

Still another adventure on a Saturday had taken them up into the cool mountain air of Ruidoso. It was there that Bob pulled to the side of the road to raise the top when a sudden summer squall had threatened to soak the two joyriders. Little Sister marveled at the power top rising mechanically and lowering back down to shield them from the rain. She thrilled to the soft pitter-patter of rainfall on the canvas roof as the couple headed on up to Billy the Kid territory at Capitan before the return drive down to the flatlands and the scorching summer heat.

And one Saturday afternoon had been spent just sitting out in the convertible with pop music being beamed into southern New Mexico from the fifty-thousand-watt KOMA radio station in Oklahoma City. That pleasant date had reminded Little Sister of a similar afternoon years earlier when Gladys and her fiancé, Deon, had brought sandwiches out from his parent's small hamburger walk-up joint called Lester's Hamburger Stand near the corner of West Tilden Street and South Pennsylvania. We Johnson kids had sat in Deon's blue and gray 1954 Ford station wagon during a steady rainfall. The closeness within the car as we sat crowded inside munching on warm burgers had managed to fog up the windows, but Deon had kept the V8 motor throbbing so the defogger fan could provide a fairly unobstructed view of the raindrops splashing off the windshield. Music from the local radio station KBIM was playing, and one song had jumped out to grab everyone's attention. It was the latest hit from Elvis Presley called "Little Sister."

And this young airman even offered a ride in his big Ford to me one Sunday afternoon after dinner was finished. We traveled a dirt road that ran along the north side parallel to the main highway to drive up to the top of Six Mile Hill for a look back to the east for a view of the distant town nestled in the Pecos River valley. He talked with me about this and that during the drive which made me feel accepted and even somehow important. As I rode shotgun along with Bob Stevens, it was easy to determine that I certainly did approve of this guy who was dating my sister.

The drive ended back at the house just in time for digging into what was left of the ritual that Momma performed Sunday afternoons—popping popcorn to fill a large, blue-speckled dishpan. Bob grabbed fistfuls of the heavily buttered and salted popcorn while I searched for the very best parts by far: the dark brown partially popped kernels at the bottom of the old oval dishpan.

Bob then walked over to stand next to the wood stove and peer through the kitchen window where he spotted Momma and Daddy sitting outside in the shade. He then wondered aloud where Gloria might be, but after strolling into the front room, he discovered her cutting out pale yellow fabric for a new summer dress.

He really seemed to be blending in quite well with the rhythms of the Johnson Sunday afternoons in the country out west of town in the area adjacent to Dogtown, out in what townsfolk almost always referred to as the "sticks." This young airman had been raised as a city boy in the very best part of Wichita, but he didn't seem to mind the primitive surroundings that made up our humble dwelling place. There was no evidence whatsoever of any disdain. Rather, this airman was fitting right in with the Johnsons!

Change was already on the wind, though, and Bob Stevens, alone, knew that any blending in with a girlfriend from out in the "sticks" was on the verge of completely evaporating into thin air.

By the second Saturday in June, Bob did not show up out at the house, neither did he appear at any of the church services on Sunday. Little Sister was obviously disappointed. What had become of her steady boyfriend? The song lyrics, "Way up high, up in the sky, oh tell me why, oh tell me why, I've lost my love" swirled around in her head for a day or two. She just couldn't help herself.

Since there was no telephone out at the house, she had not received a call from him. She rather quickly determined that he had been transferred. Was he moved out to another duty assignment, maybe even to another base? Had he been denied any opportunity to even offer a proper goodbye?

But it was the next Friday night while cruising Main Street with Cindy, my girlfriend during my last two years of high school, that I spotted him. The red convertible turned off Main onto the entrance to the drive-in picture show just as my big Plymouth approached from behind in the northward traffic flow. I was shocked! There was no mistaking what I had seen first-hand under the bright streetlights. Snuggled up right next to Bob was a young woman with curly blond hair. His right arm was casually draped over her shoulders as they motored along.

I successfully managed to stifle my reaction to the grim discovery. Luckily, Cindy had not noticed the offending sight at all.

Bob's betrayal of Gloria remained my tightly kept secret. In my judgement, my sister would do well to simply remember him as she had briefly known him and to just keep believing that his complete vanishing was something the Air Force sometimes did with personnel.

She seemed content enough within a few weeks to just chalk it all up to happenstance, and continued throughout the remaining months of that summer with the available support and comfort to be found in the words of Momma's favorite hymn,

FARTHER ALONG WE'LL KNOW ALL ABOUT IT,

FARTHER ALONG WE'LL UNDERSTAND WHY.

CHEER UP, MY BROTHER, LIVE IN THE SUNSHINE,

WE'LL UNDERSTAND IT ALL BY AND BY.

Besides, Little Sister had certainly never intended to fall head over heels in love with him, anyway!

10   A HATCHET FOR BURYING

"Wouldn't you at least agree that many things are better left unsaid and just left alone entirely?

Why are you determined to say things to make this life way out here so much worse than it already is?

What is it that seems to drive you to constantly put me down instead of focusing on finding anything you could complement me with?

When, exactly, did I cease from being your dutiful, obedient daughter that you always demanded?

Why do you constantly mock me when I stumble in word or deed but fail to take your own actions into account?

Why do you still call me Little Sister now that I've been away to college, and you have young Geneva at home?"

Those six questions, and many, many more along with various observations more general in nature can be found in her journal that began back when she was in her sophomore year of high school. And even though each entry seems poisonous, at least upon a casual reading, deeper and more difficult emotions are tightly wrapped up in every heartfelt writing at the time of recording them in the journal. Retrospective reflection on the intended meaning of each entry is, naturally, subject to debate and perhaps adjustment as well. Overall, though, her life was clearly anything but pleasant during those years if the questions and observations are taken strictly at face value.

A strong indictment could possibly be made about the perceived failure of the curriculum presented during her years of study at Houston Bible College followed by a lengthy ministry internship up near Schenectady, New York. Shouldn't something in that time have served to eradicate any harbored resentment or withheld forgiveness of her father? Wasn't a true change of heart to be expected from exposure to all the genuinely godly precepts that most assuredly were expounded in environments of that nature?

But as it all turned out, a very sharp hatchet had been raised against her pretty much as soon as Little Sister, now Gloria to everyone but Daddy, returned to Auto Route West from New York. She bristled at the treatment she received after several years of being free from such awful negativity, so scores of new journal entries were added to the already bursting volume. Try as she might, victory over the tumultuous relationship with her father and the profound mistreatment she endured was not forthcoming. She wanted a brand-new start. She *needed* a brand-new start. She needed to just get out, and soon.

As Gloria would later put it, the straw that finally "broke the camel's back" came one evening just after the sun had set and Daddy had mercilessly berated her for not washing and drying the supper dishes the way he thought they should have been done. It was a tremendously petty thing to get all riled up about, but he had. Her young twelve-year-old sister, Geneva, had watched from afar as the awkward situation had unfolded and cried when it became abundantly clear that her big sister Gloria had had enough and just could not possibly take another minute of such completely unnecessary verbal abuse.

The situation was puzzling to Geneva. Just why was Daddy always so hard on Gloria?

She was, however, certainly content to keep the real security of her own position within the family structure as the baby sister who really couldn't do anything wrong in her Daddy's eyes. It was the very same position, unbeknownst to Geneva, that had once belonged to the one who was now departing in haste.

Withdrawing exactly four nickels in loose change from her purse, Gloria slipped the coins into her skirt pocket and set her purse back down, quickly hugged her sister, and walked out the kitchen door as if to simply head out to the facilities outdoors. Instead, she kept walking north alongside Brown Road until she reached Woody's Truck Stop up at the highway on West Second. Her only call was to the parsonage of the church where the Johnsons regularly attended. After telling the pastor's wife her side of the situation and asking if she could spend the night at their home, she sat down on an outside bench adjacent to the telephone booth to await the arrival of the pastor and his wife.

It was then that a blue pickup stopped opposite of her position. The driver's window was rolled down and his voice was loud enough for her to clearly understand his offer of a ride if she wanted one.

The young brown-headed guy quickly added that he had a few cans of cold Schlitz beer just waiting for them.

She politely declined the offer of a ride by calmly stating that she was waiting for her pastor to come for her. Upon that news, the young "Pick-Up-Man" very quickly picked up and drove away!

By the following day Gloria had managed to secure appropriate lodging, where a spare bedroom in the large home of one of the long-time church families became her new living space.

Riding out with that host family the next morning to pick up her purse and other belongings, she was met just inside the front door and asked only one question by Daddy,

"Can't we just bury the hatchet?"

"No! I just can't right now," was the response as she continued though the length of the house to gather her things from the back bedroom.

A young man named Cecil was still living in the house with his parents and apparently figured that he would be a shoo-in for courting Gloria, the new female guest resident in their home. But what a major miscalculation that had been! Gloria found him to be extremely disgusting in so many ways. Not only was he overweight for a twenty-two-year-old but was downright ugly with fresh acne scars covering much of his face and neck. And besides, who would ever name someone Cecil, anyway?

The marriage of Gloria and Doug took place inside the Roswell home of his parents, the Lamontines. Since the groom had shown appropriate behavior by asking if he could have Gloria for his bride, the ice between the father and daughter and his future son-in-law had already started to melt. And when it was time for giving the bride away, Gloria readily accepted her father's offer. The former Little Sister looked deeply into her father's eyes and stated,

"Yes! And we can finally bury that hatchet, too!"

Daddy then exalted,

"Well, it's a great big beautiful sunshiny day!"

So, all those years of Christian education down in Texas and the work experience up in New York had certainly paid off after all!

www.ingramcontent.com/pod-product-compliance
Lightning Source LLC
Chambersburg PA
CBHW051325120626
46547CB00015B/2399